THE GREEN WITCH GARDEN

ARY

LITTLE BOOK OF CANDLE MAGIC

BY EMBER LIVINGSTON EMMONS

THE GREEN WITCH GARDEN APOTHECARY

LITTLE BOOK OF CANDLE MAGIC

BY EMBER LIVINGSTON EMMONS

THE GREEN WITCH GARDEN APOTHECARY

LITTLE BOOK OF CANDLE MAGIC

BY

EMBER LIVINGSTON EMMONS

WWW.GREENWITCHGARDENAPOTHECARY.COM

CONTENTS:

WITH LOVE.

CANDLE MAGIC

EVERY SINGLE STEP BEGINS WITH AN INTENTION.

LET THE POWER OF MINDFUL INTENTION MAKE MAGIC IN YOUR LIFE.

USING CANDLES FOR MEDITATION ALLOWS YOUR GAZE AN ACTIVE PLACE TO REST, A FOCUSED, PRESENT AND INTENTIONAL WAY TO ALLOW YOUR INTUITION ITS VOICE.

MAKE YOUR INTENTIONS AS SPECIFIC AS POSSIBLE, WRITE THEM DOWN, OR HOLD THEM IN YOUR MIND BEFORE LIGHTING THE CANDLE. AS THE CANDLE RELEASES IT'S ENERGY (IT IS MADE WITH POWERFUL LOVING INTENTIONS AND FILLED WITH PLANT MAGIC, ENFOLDED IN THE WAX OF BEES), ALLOW YOUR INTENTIONS TO BE RELEASED, YOU CAN FEEL FREE TO LET YOUR MIND DRIFT AND EMPTY WHILE THE CANDLE BURNS. IF YOU HAVE BEEN STUCK IN AN AREA, USING THIS MINDFUL, INTENTIONAL ACTION CAN CAUSE POWERFUL SHIFTS.

"To create out of love, that love has to extend to yourself. Love is an action. Meditation is the commitment to the action of self-love."

-Green Witch Garden Apothecary

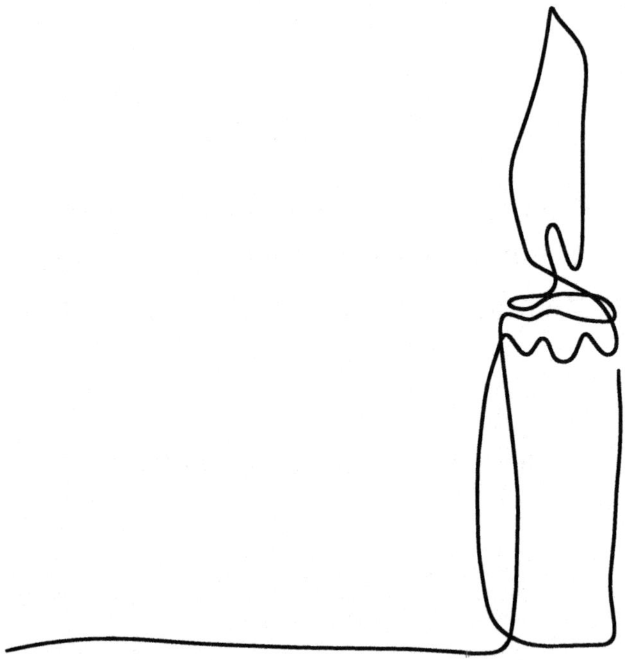

INTENTION CANDLES ARE A BEAUTIFUL, VIBRANT CREATIVE OUTLET THAT ARE A MEANINGFUL WAY TO PROMOTE PEACE, LOVE AND LIGHT IN THE WORLD.

EACH INTENTION CANDLE I LIGHT IS A LITTLE PROMISE TO MYSELF: I AM STARTING THE PROCESS, I SIGNAL TO MY UNCONSCIOUS. I AM LIGHTING THE FLAME OF ACTION. ACTION IS ENERGY; ENERGY IS ALWAYS HAPPENING. YES, MEDITATION IS ABOUT BEING STILL, RESTING THE MIND AND GIVING YOUR DEEP CONSCIOUSNESS (I CALL IT INTUITION) THE SPACE IT NEEDS TO PROCESS AND INFORM THE PARTS OF YOUR BRAIN THAT MAKES DECISIONS.

FACT: YOU CANNOT EXPECT TO OPERATE YOUR HUMAN BEING BODY AT AN OPTIMUM LEVEL UNLESS YOU OPERATE IT AT AN OPTIMUM. IF YOUR NERVOUS SYSTEM IS RESPONDING TO UNRELEASED TRAUMA, YOU MAY BE LITERALLY LOCKED INTO A CYCLE OF SURVIVAL.

When I light a candle, I am promising to tend to myself. I am promising to pay attention to what I want, and where I am paying attention (where your attention goes, the energy flows!).

Can I meditate without a candle? Yes, of course, and I do- but I am much more focused and less likely to drift in a "busy" way when I have the pretty flame to gaze at. How the candle melts, shimmers, the show of the plants and wax as it burns, all of these are active, beautiful creation in action!

I picture each candle as an energy cleansing machine. There's so much love and power in them that they literally combust bad energy and transform it into light.

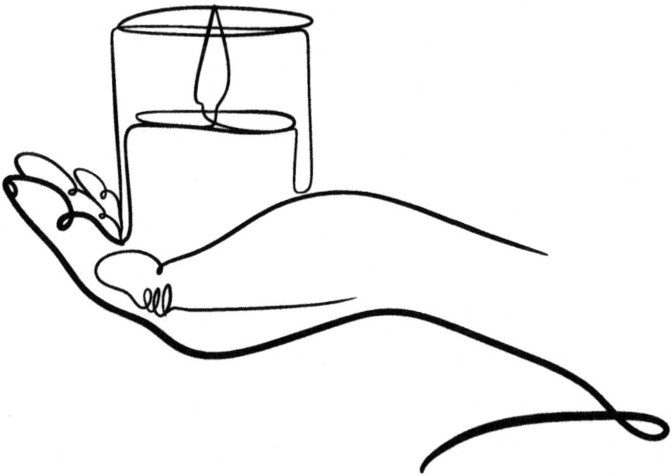

MAKING YOUR OWN INTENTION/SPELL CANDLES

Equipment:

As you probably know, as with anything, there is no limit to how fancy and extensive you can get with equipment. However, if you're just making some intention candles for your own use, you really do not need much to get going.

Note: you can certainly repurpose household items for wax work, but once you do, it's much better if that is designated only for wax. Wax is incredibly difficult to get out of stuff- even metal. There's some tips at the end for how to remove wax from various surfaces, but the lingering wax feel is really hard to get rid of. You'll taste it forever. It's like mincing garlic in a food processor but worse.

That being said...

You can literally start with a soup can if that's what you have. It's a perfect little inner double boiler piece, and you can save it to keep using it, or throw it away each time.

If at all possible, put it in a bigger pot that you don't have to use again to cook with. I am really serious about this one. At the least, you can designate one small saucepan to use with soup cans, and you can store this with the lid on and everything you used to stir the wax inside.
The next step up, and where I started, was with a tiny sauce sized crock-pot. It worked great for a long time. If each intention candle is about an ounce, a little 2 cup crock actually makes a good batch of candles, and possibly even more than you have molds for.

There are also melting kettles that are attached to their own little heat source.

The downsides of a kettle melter or melting directly in a small small crock pot is that it somewhat limits your options for color, and it reduces the time you have to infuse the wax as you don't want to have any plant matter in the wax if it's in a heating source directly, as this increases the risk of fire. Direct heat is much more important to track than wax in a double boiler, where the heat is distributed much more evenly.

The good part is that it keeps melting separate from your cooking stove, and I cannot stress how nice this is.

I currently use a combination of methods, but at any given hour, you will find my giant crock pot full of various designated mason jars immersed in lavender florasol on very low heat. This way, I can keep colors separate when I am using dyes that require a higher melting temperature to get the richest colors.

THIS ISN'T THE CASE FOR MICA POWDERS AND LIQUID MIX-IN DYES, WHICH TAKE NO TIME TO DEVELOP, AND CAN BE MIXED INTO WAX AFTER IT'S REMOVED FROM THE HEAT, JUST BEFORE POURING. THIS IS A REALLY GOOD WAY TO MAKE MICRO-BATCHES OF SPECIFIC COLORS.

ONCE YOUR WAX IS MELTED, YOU'LL NEED SOME STICKS OR UTENSILS TO STIR IT WITH, AND TO MIX THE COLORS. I USE "WAX WANDS" OF THIN BAMBOO THAT I CUT ABOUT 8 INCHES LONG. THE THIN BAMBOO ALSO FITS INTO MY MICA, AND SO I USE THE WANDS FOR COLOR, TOO.
A POPSICLE STICK WOULD WORK, OR A SPOON OR CHOPSTICKS DONATED TO THE CAUSE.

To really choose the best method to melt your wax, you should first choose your wax. Different wax have different combustion temperatures, and you have to be careful not to get wrong wax too hot. Hot wax is dangerous, burn burning wax is deadly. Not only is it extremely flammable as it gets too hot, it also begins to emit toxic fumes. Your wax should never be smoking.

I use 100% Beeswax in my intention candles exclusively at this time, but I do like to experiment with other waxes for other types of candles. There is not another wax that is as good to burn as beeswax, in my opinion, but there are other blends that might throw more scent, cost less or take color more easily.

Soy Wax is a good second, because it is sustainable, burns and melts nicely, and actually takes color and scent better than beeswax in some cases.

There are many other types of waxes, the most common being paraffin. Paraffin is a petroleum derivative, so while it does throw scents well and hold shape and color, I don't want to use them.

There are many types of plant waxes, but the extraction processes are intense, and some use petroleum products in the process of extraction, which makes them less attractive for me to want to burn/breathe. This isn't true of every wax, so just make sure to read about the source of the wax to know what's in it. There is no question that Beeswax burns the cleanest.

Coconut wax is also a popular common wax, but almost all that you find will be a soy blend.

I will sometimes add coconut oil or other oils to my beeswax for scent or to make it softer.
My favorites are Tomato seed and peach kernel.
Both are quite expensive but make a lovely blend.

When you've chosen your wax and how you're going to melt it, It's time to choose a mold, or a heat-proof container that you can pour the wet wax directly into with a wick.

My favorite candle are the ones I make with molds that I create myself. After much experimentation, I now make almost all my molds out of pourable silicone, but there are many other creative options. AN ice-cube tray is a great mold for quickly making a batch of small candles. The silicone type of ice tray is the easiest, and there are lots of fun shapes and sizes on the market. The old-fashioned kind of ice-trays work fine, too.

You can pour wax Directly into nut shells, sea-shells and egg-shells, add a wick, and burn them just like that after a little curing time. Or, you can "peel" the shells off the hardened wax.

METAL CONTAINERS OR JARS CAN BE USED, JUST SECURE A WICK TO THE BOTTOM AND THEN FILL THEM WITH WET WAX. PRETTY GLASSES, TEACUPS, RICE OR PINCH BOWLS AND TERRA COTTA POTS ARE ALL LOVELY TO POUR CANDLES DIRECTLY INTO. YOU CAN ALSO PURCHASE PACKS OF LITTLE METAL TEA-LIGHT CONTAINERS, OFTEN WITH WICKS INCLUDED.

IF YOU OPT FOR FREE STANDING CANDLES, THERE ARE MANY GORGEOUS MOLDS OUT THERE, AND IF YOU SEE AN OBJECT THAT YOU KNOW WOULD MAKE THE PERFECT CANDLE. MAKE YOUR OWN SILICONE MOLD, IT'S EASY AND FUN!

Tip: Silicone molds don't last forever, so if you find or make one you especially love, make sure to cast a "hard copy" that you can use again to make new molds. I like to use two-part epoxy for this, as it creates a hard, permanent model that I can use again and again.

Choose a wick that is a few inches longer than your candle will be. There are a few ways to secure a wick in a container so that it will stay where you want it in a candle. Many wicks come with double sided stickers, but I don't want to breathe those if they get hot, so I don't use them. Instead, I like using a popsicle stick with a small hole drilled through it, so that I can hang the wick in the center of the candle. With a silicone mold, I will thread the wick through a tiny hole in the bottom of the mold for this purpose. Be careful with this, as wax really wanders if given a chance, and too big a hole will wreck your mold.

Always thread or hang your wick first- even a waxed wick will melt if you push it into hot wax, but it will stay where it is if the wax is poured around it.

IT'S GOOD TO USE A METAL WICK STABILIZER FOR MOST CANDLES; IN A JAR, THE WICK CAN FLOAT WHEN ALL THE WAX IS MELTED IF IT ISN'T SECURED.

MANY PRE-WAXED WICKS COME WITH METAL TABS, OR METAL TABS CAN BE PURCHASED IN PACKS IF YOU'RE USING UNWAXED WICKING AND CUTTING YOUR OWN.

I'VE ALSO USED A METAL WASHER OR YOU CAN DRILL A HOLD IN A METAL DISC OF ANY SORT, USE A POP-CAN TAB, OR A PAPER-CLIP.

ADDITIONS: SCENTS, PLANTS & CRYSTALS

No matter what anyone tells you, nothing is going to "bind" with the beeswax. What will happen is that the oils/additives will distribute evenly through the melted wax. They will also separate if they get a chance.

Water will not incorporate at all.

Beeswax will never go bad; what could cause mold over time is moisture in the wax. This can come from additives, like plants that aren't dried well enough. Essential oils, especially, lose their fragrance at temps below candle burning, or even some wax melting, depending on the oils.

Most candles are scented with "fragrance oils" which may be completely or partly synthetic.

THE TERM "THROW" DESCRIBES THE SCENT A CANDLE GIVES OFF. THERE ARE SCIENTIFIC MEASURES OF THIS, BUT AS THE WORD IS COMMONLY USED, THIS CAN BE VERY SUBJECTIVE. THE COLD THROW REFERS TO THE SCENT OF A CANDLE WHEN IT IS UNLIT, AND THE HOT THROW IS THE SCENT WHEN LIT.

WHEN YOU'RE DECIDING HOW MUCH AND OF WHAT TYPE OF FRAGRANCE YOU USE FOR A CANDLE, IT'S HELPFUL TO BE MINDFUL OF WHAT THE CANDLE WILL BE USED FOR, AND WHERE. I PERSONALLY GET HEADACHES VERY EASILY FROM FRAGRANCE OIL, AND WALKING DOWN THE DETERGENT AISLE CAN GIVE ME A MIGRAINE, SO I USE A VERY LIMITED SELECTION OF OILS. I MUCH PREFER TO RENDER OIL FROM PLANTS, LIKE I RENDER ESSENCES BY DISTILLING.

I AM ALSO GOING TO USE INTENTION CANDLES TO MEDITATE, INDOORS, AND I REALLY LIKE A FRESH, BEAUTIFUL CANDLE AT LEAST EACH DAY. I DON'T WANT TOO STRONG OF A SCENT, ESPECIALLY AN ARTIFICIAL ONE.

Be really careful with floral scents. They can easily overpower. There is a lot more margin for error with sharper, herbal, minty or lemon/citrus-y oils in my opinion.

When I am scenting wax, I consider how it will be used, and layer the scents accordingly. The main use of my intention candles are to fire my creativity and focus while I work- like a background of intention, and to use for meditation. The last thing I want during either of these activities is to go off on a scent. So, I layer a heavier cold throw, which is nice for focus (and nice when I make and handle the wax and candles) that is light and fresh, with a minimal hot throw.

As the candle heats up, the fragrance will mellow out, allowing the natural beeswax scent to be dominant. This keeps me happy for longer periods of concentration.

I love to add dried and fresh plants to my intention candles. Before I go deeper into that, I want to make it clear that an intention candle is meant for contemplation; it is never to be left unattended.

Most of my candles are free-standing or contained in tin. I play with a lot of beautiful candle holders, but it's very difficult for me to find one that I feel comfortable selling. I use them, but I am very mindful that these are candles intended for attending to. Almost all glass will shatter if it gets hot enough. Wax ignites when it gets hot enough. The added plants are potentially fire-starters. I only add them to candles intended to be intention candles and watched very closely.

If a candle is in a glass container, be mindful about how much plant material you add, and what type. It can collect in the bottom and catch fire, and the glass will break. I have a couple marble slabs that I burn all my candles on.

I never set them on the counter or a table without a slab of something heat-proof under it.

Even metal gets hot enough to burn wood under it.

For intention candles, the plants burn and add a little drama to the show. The put off some smoke, which is a nice aroma without overpowering.

My favorite plants to add are:

Cacao

Love, peace, compassion

Calendula

prophetic dreams, protection. for the sacral chakra.

Chamomile

Purification, Sleep, Rest and Meditation. Removes curses. Carry on person to attract money and abundance. Use in steam for romance, use on skin for luck.

Clove

Protection, Love, Money, banishment of negative thoughts.

Lavender

Love, sleep, depression, psychic abilities and SOOTHING.
For the crown and heart chakras.

Mullein

Courage, Protection, Divination, Health.

Mugwort

The Beautiful Dreamer: use for prophetic dreams.

Nettle

Exorcism, Protection, Healing; Lust. Use for the heart Chakra.

Rose Petals

Love, purification and trust. Beauty, passion and love.
Anti-anxiety, luck, positive energy.
Offer roses for friendly spirits. Symbol Magic.

REMEMBER TO ONLY USE CANDLES IN VERY WELL VENTILATED AREAS!

USE ONLY A VERY SMALL AMOUNT OF PLANT MATTER TO BURN, USE MORE CEREMONIALLY AROUND THE CANDLE, BUT BREATHE AS LITTLE SMOKE AS POSSIBLE. THE POWER IS IN THE INTENTION.

Rocks and crystals can be powerful and beautiful additions, just make sure you know what you are including. Some crystals are not suited to hot temperature and will shatter or burn.

When I add crystals and rocks, I don't put them in a direct line of the wick, but more around the perimeter, at various layers, to reveal themselves as the wax heats.

Some of my favorites to add are:

Aventurine
Quartz,
Rose Quartz

Candles don't need any additional colorants, but adding them can add beauty and meaning to the candles.
Colorants can be added to melting wax on heat, or stirred in after, as mentioned earlier, depending on what you're working on.

Wax colorants: vegetable wax based dyes that melt with the wax. Check the temps on these, as many do not melt at the same temp as beeswax, and the beeswax will discolor and overheat before the color melts. These colors are usually solid and intense, depending on the concentration. They usually don't have a shimmer to them.

Mica- Can be metallic or pearly, is powdered and can be stirred into the wax at any point, or dusted into the drying wax. Be careful not to breathe it loose. This is usually more sparkly, and allows more of the natural color to show through. Too much mica can clog the wick of a candle, so use sparingly, especially in a larger candle or a candle in a container.

Spices, flowers and vegetables are also good ways to add color (and scent) to beeswax.

Cinnamon, nutmeg or cloves both scent and color.

Rose petals or other flower petals can be melted in the wax and strained out (or not).

Raspberries, beets, spinach or onion skins can be steeped in the melting wax to add some tinting.

Candle Magic & Color Symbolism

RED CANDLES:

THE ROOT CHAKRA. COURAGE, VITALITY, ENERGY, ACTION, LUST, SEXUAL ENERGY.

ORANGE CANDLES:

THE SACRAL CHAKRA. SUCCESS, AMBITION, CELEBRATION, OPPORTUNITY, JUSTICE

YELLOW CANDLES:

THE SOLAR PLEXUS CHAKRA. INTELLIGENCE, CLARITY, JOY, MEMORY, REASON

GREEN CANDLES:

THE HEART CHAKRA. LOVE, ABUNDANCE, MANIFESTATION, GROWTH, PHYSICAL HEALTH

BLUE CANDLES:

LIGHT BLUE: THE THROAT CHAKRA.. COMMUNICATION, FORGIVENESS, POWER PSYCHIC ABILITY.

INDIGO CANDLES:

DARK BLUE: THIRD EYE CHAKRA. HIDDEN KNOWLEDGE, WISDOM, PSYCHIC ABILITY.

PURPLE CANDLES:

THE CROWN CHAKRA. DEVELOPMENT, AUTHORITY, INFLUENCE, SPIRITUAL CONNECTION

BROWN CANDLES:

EARTH MAGIC. HOUSE MAGIC.
BLESSINGS.

BLACK CANDLES:

SAFETY, PROTECTION,
BANISHING NEGATIVITY,
SHADOW CARE, ABUNDANCE.

WHITE CANDLES:

DIVINATION, EXORCISM.

WAX FACTS

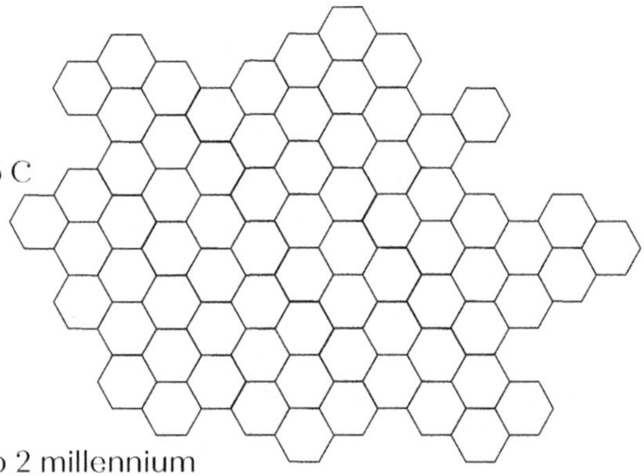

Beeswax

Melting Point: 144-150 F, 62-65 C

Discolors: 170 F, 77 C

Add Oils: 160-165 F, 71-74

Pour: 140-150 F, 60-65 C

Flash Point: 400 F, 204.4 C

Cure time: 2 days to 2 weeks to 2 millennium

Soy Wax

Melting Point: 1113-127 F, 45-53 C

Discolors: 170 F, 77 C

Add Oils: 180-185 F, 82-85 C

Pour: 120-140 F, 48-60 C

Flash Point: 450 F, 232 C

Cure time: 3 days to 2 weeks

Melting the wax:

Choose something you can dedicate to wax, including the appliance itself if at all possible- like a crockpot, dedicated electric pot, hot plate, etc).

Double-boiling helps insulate the wax from overheating and overheating on the heat source. If you're using a direct heat source, like a crock-pot, it's better to partially fill the crock with water and melt your wax in glass or metal containers submerged in the water.

Choose a melting container, can, stainless pitcher, etc. I like jars and silicone cups- cover and keep clean, and keep colors apart.

WHATEVER METHOD YOU'RE USING TO MELT YOUR WAX, KEEP YOUR THERMOMETER CLOSE AND KEEP AN EYE ON THAT TEMP. OVERHEATING WAX CAN BE DANGEROUS. ONCE IT IGNITES, IT IS VERY HARD TO PUT OUT.

IF YOU WAX DOES IGNITE: DO NOT PUT WATER ON IT.

THIS WILL MAKE IT 100 TIMES WORSE, AND WILL PROBABLY CAUSE IT TO INJURE YOU AND SPREAD EVEN MORE QUICKLY.

IT'S A GOOD IDEA TO MAKE SURE YOU HAVE A HOUSEHOLD CHEMICAL FIRE EXTINGUISHER HANDY, BUT YOU CAN EXTINGUISH A WAX FIRE WITH BAKING SODA ALSO.

BEYOND BEING A FIRE HAZARD, THERE ARE OTHER REASONS TO WATCH THE TEMPERATURE. YOU SHOULD WORK WITH THE WAX AS COOL AS POSSIBLE. OVER ABOUT 170 F, WAX CAN DISCOLOR, AND IT LOSES IT'S SCENT.

I LIKE TO MELT THE WAX SLOWLY, AND NEVER TURN MY CROCK POT ABOVE THE LOWEST KEEP WARM SETTING. YOU CAN DEFINITELY USE WATER TO DOUBLE BOIL/MELT WAX. I USE DISTILLED LAVENDER FLORASOL, BECAUSE I MAKE IT AND IT ADDS AN EXTRA LAYER OF INTENTION/PLANT MAGIC TO MY CANDLES. IT ALSO MAKES AN AROMA THAT MAKES ME SUPER HAPPY AND RELAXED, WHICH MAKES THE CANDLES HAVE BETTER ENERGY.

Keep an eye on the temperature, and add the scents/ oils according the the type of wax you're using.

Add any other additions after the wax is removed from the heat, as different materials have different flash points than the wax alone, and can catch fire. When the wax is clear of heat, I stir in my plant medley as it cools, and in some cases, I'll just add my herbs directly to the mold before I pour the wax in.

There is a magic to pouring beeswax- the cooler the better, but one degree too cool and it doesn't pour well. This matters more in a mold, and as you experiment, you'll get the feel for it.

POUR THE WAX AS SLOWLY AND EVENLY AS POSSIBLE, AND GIVE THE CONTAINER A FEW LIGHT TAPS AS YOU GO TO HELP ELIMINATE AS MANY BUBBLES AS POSSIBLE. I WILL POUR, TAP TAP TAP, WAIT A SEC FOR IT TO SETTLE, POUR A BIT MORE TO TOP IT OFF AGAIN, AND REPEAT UNTIL THE WAX FORMS A FILM AND IS NO LONGER WET. AT THIS POINT, IT WILL NOT STICK EFFECTIVELY. SO KEEP THAT IN MIND.

WET WAX STICKS TO WET WAX, BUT JUST LIKE IT WON'T BIND WITH OILS OR WATER, IT ALSO WON'T BIND WITH FIRM WAX- IT WILL HARDEN SEPARATELY AND YOUR CANDLE WILL COME APART IN PIECES WITH NOT MUCH FORCE. THIS IS FINE FOR SOME CANDLES, BUT DEPENDING ON YOUR END-USE, NOT FOR OTHER APPLICATIONS.

Once a film has formed on the wax, let it sit for at least a few hours to harden before de-molding, if you're using a mold. Then the candle can be stored in a cool, dark (hopefully dust-free) place where it can cure.

For a large candle, a pillar candle or a candle in a jar or container, I let them cure for longer than a candle that I expect to burn free-standing.

A very loose guideline is a day per ounce to cure.

MEDITATION

THE BASICS

1.

SET YOUR INTENTIONS FOR THE MEDITATION. ARE YOU DEVOTING THIS TIME TO RELAXING? TO CONSCIOUSLY DE-STRESSING AND RELEASING YOUR NERVOUS SYSTEM? ARE YOU WORKING TO ACCOMPLISH A SPECIFIC GOAL, OR TO UNDERSTAND A SITUATION? IT DOESN'T HAVE TO BE A COMPLICATED INTENTION- IT CAN BE AS SIMPLE AS "SEEKING CLARITY" OR "LISTENING FOR INTUITION".

3.

CHOOSE A TIME A SPACE WHERE YOU WILL BE MINIMALLY INTERRUPTED FOR THE MEDITATION. IT'S OKAY TO MAKE A MEDITATION ONE MINUTE LONG- BUT BE COMPLETELY FOCUSED AND INTENTIONAL FOR THAT ONE MINUTE. GIVE IT YOUR ABSOLUTE ALL, AND THAT'S MORE IMPORTANT THAN TIME SPENT. THAT BEING SAID, THE LONGER THE BETTER FOR RELAXING AND LETTING STRESS GO.

Candle Meditations

CHOOSE THE CANDLE FOR YOUR INTENTION. CHOOSE A CANDLE ACCORDING TO COLOR, SHAPE, AND INGREDIENTS TO CREATE THE LIGHT YOU NEED TO GIVE LIFE TO THE INTENTIONS. REMEMBER- A WHITE CANDLE CAN FILL IN FOR ANY OTHER COLOR, AND IF YOU DON'T HAVE A SELECTION HANDY, YOU CAN WORK WITH WHAT YOU HAVE. THE CANDLE DOESN'T HAVE THE POWER- YOU DO, AND YOU GIVE IT TO THE CANDLE.

Safety First!

*Always trim wick to 1/8"-1/4" before lighting for best burning.

1. Always place candle in a fire-proof container, on a heat-resistant surface.

Keep all loose fabrics and papers away from burning area. Never leave a candle unattended.

UNDERSTAND THAT MEDITATION IS A NOT A REPLACEMENT FOR MEDICAL TREATMENT. GET PROPER MEDICAL CARE FOR ANY MENTAL HEALTH ISSUES, INCLUDING MEDICATION WHEN THAT IS APPROPRIATE. MEDITATE WHILE MAKING THE BEST DECISIONS FOR YOURSELF- NEVER INSTEAD OF, AS THIS IS COMPLETELY CONTRARY TO THE PURPOSE OF MEDITATION. MEDITATION IS COMMITMENT TO SELF-LOVE, AS IS MAKING SURE YOU'RE RECEIVING PROPER MEDICAL CARE WHEN YOU NEED IT.

GET COMFORTABLE. CHOOSE A WELL VENTILATED AREA WHERE YOU CAN SIT COMFORTABLY. IT'S OKAY TO SIT IN A CHAIR OR ON THE FLOOR. KEEP THE CANDLE WITHIN EASY REACH, WHERE YOU CAN COMFORTABLE GAZE AT IT. WEAR CLOTHING THAT DOESN'T BIND.

HAVE PLENTY OF DRINKING WATER AT YOUR SIDE. HERBAL TISANES OR TEAS ARE ALSO A NICE OPTION.

If there are objects or rituals that are sacred to you, incorporate them. The more emotion, love and joy you imbue the candle burning with, the more effective it will be. Plants, rocks or other natural items are a way to incorporate your oneness with nature, and can be powerful additions.

Some people like to write their intention, or what they'd like to release, before lighting the candle, and then add them to the flame one by one. It's also fine to take a moment and set your intentions mentally or aloud before lighting the candle, in lieu of writing on paper.

If you do chose to burn your intention, keep the papers as small as possible-a word or phrase that's representative is good! Make sure you're in an area that is ventilated. There is no smoke inhale that's good for your lungs. We purify the air and cleanse energy with candles and plants, but we only ever breath fresh, smoke-free air.

Ideally, allow the candle to determine how long a meditation goes. Single use intention candles rarely go longer than 30 minutes, and generally are closer to 25. But, set a timer if you must- as gently as possible.

Some people prefer wooden matches, or a lighting stick, but that's your preference. As you watch the candle, be aware of your breathing.
Take long, slow breaths through your nose (do not be in a closed room breathing smoke! Ventilate!), and even slower, longer breaths out through your mouth.

You can happily muse about your intentions as you watch the candle fire dance and play, if it feels good, or just listen to the flicker of the flame, or repeat a mantra or affirmation. This time can be used for tapping, switch words, or any other positive, preferably bilateral and repetitive action, if it feels good and helps to stay focused. Music is wonderful but try to avoid lyrics. Focus on your own story.

.IF YOU FIND YOUR MIND HAS DRIFTED, YOU CAN USE THIS AS A REMINDER TO CHECK YOUR BODY FOR TENSION. RELEASE YOUR JAW, NECK, SHOULDERS, TAILBONE AND KEGEL MUSCLES.
ALLOW YOUR BELLY TO RELEASE AS YOUR SPINE NATURALLY GROWS, ALLOWING ALL YOUR ORGANS THEIR FULL SPACE, AND ROOM FOR DEEPER, SLOWER BREATHS.

FOR DRIFTING MIND: ARE THE THOUGHTS PLEASANT, AND MAKE YOU FEEL GOOD TO THINK ABOUT? GOOD! KEEP THINKING THEM, AND GET AS EXCITED AS YOU CAN! SMILE AND LAUGH, IF YOU FEEL LIKE IT, TAP YOUR FINGERS, WIGGLE YOUR TOES. IF YOU'RE PLEASANTLY IMMERSED IN IMAGINING THINGS THAT BRING YOU JOY- PLANNING HOW GREAT SOME MOMENT WILL FEEL, THE PROCESSES OF GETTING THERE- YOUR OSCAR ACCEPTANCE SPEECH (: WHATEVER FEELS GOOD, GET CARRIED AWAY WITH IT.

For intrusive thoughts- If the thoughts are stressful or worrisome, or your mind has just wandered to the mundane, do a body scan, first, relaxing your muscles. Try to focus so intently on loosening the muscles in your body, especially around the tailbone and jaw. I focus on releasing as intently as I possibly can, focusing every bit of attention and intention on the muscle.

It's loosening as hard as you can, if you will- and if you can loosen intently enough, you may find your body will shiver, shake a little, get tickly, goosebumps, and other physical sensations. Allow it as much as possible! Go with it, shake it out. Those shivers will never manifest in fear based behaviors again, allow yourself joy in the process.

Visualization.

Create a mental anchor, it will be a key to your sanctuary when you need it. Make it as clear and visceral as you can- a super familiar object like an apple or a tree are perfect for visualization exercises. Expend your energy conjuring a mental picture- really focus on it. The better you get at this, the easier it will be to find that anchor when you need it.

Listen...

Just listen to connect to the infinite.

Listen to something beautiful, something inspiring- or just listen; is there a refrigerator running, or an air conditioner? Traffic in the distance? Listen to it. Listen as closely as you can. Don't judge, just let it be, and listen. Everything has a sound, a vibration. Hold an empty cup to your ear and listen. When you listen, you hear the OM with your intuition. It grounds and centers.

When you listen, you hear where you need the healing.

Allow the process to happen. Allow the layers to unfold.

Tips:

Use a mantra. Any word or simple phrase works, or even counting will do the trick. Just say it or think it over and over. Louder if you have to.
Move your body. Give yourself a physical task. Hold your arms out straight out to your sides as you watch the candle. Or, hold a squat, lightly bouncing. Planks require full attention.

Use a physical grounding tool, like a spray or anything you can physically live in the moment. Dry tea bags to smell, beads, or, our favorite, good for the skin florasols. Aim for causing and noticing pleasant physical sensations, and training your body and mind to focus in the present. Plus, it can be comforting, smell nice, and good for your skin.

Drink water. I incorporate this into a daily ritual. My number one and two non-negotiables in a day are be aware of breathing at least once, and to drink enough water. I have tied meditative habits into these daily necessities, which makes it so I never go a day without actively practicing my commitment to honoring my wellbeing. For me, I mentally Om whenever I'm drinking water. I breathe with affirmations, and I actively listen for Om when I brush my teeth.

Knit, crochet, play with play dough or clay. Prayer beads, crystals or stones are also a good way to direct energy physically.

When my thoughts are super negative, repetitive and really hard to shake, and I can't get something more fun to work first, I will get something else stuck in my head. Sometimes the leap from intrusive to affirmation is too much. A thought is an action. It is hard to go from lying flat to standing up in one move. It is easier to first roll on your side, then kneel, etc.

Keep at it!

Breath Magic

Breathing is connection.

Breath flows through all of us.
It connects us,
nourishes us, heals us all.

GUIDED BREATHING WORKS WONDERS FOR SOME PEOPLE, BUT FOR ALL PEOPLE, JUST TAKING THE TIME TO NOTICE AND APPRECIATE THE BREATH THAT FLOWS IN AND OUT, INCREASES CALM AND HELPS GROUND AND FOCUS.

Our minds get in the way of our bodies releasing stress. It's stored in our bodies, and spills over in ways that can hurt us, physically, mentally and spiritually.

Meditation allows the body, mind and spirit the space it needs to release the body and allow your energetic self to emerge with power and love.

The mind lies, and the brain listens.
It causes the body to react to emotions and stress,
positive and negative.

The body is the ultimate sanctuary.
Don't let the mind rob you of that truth.
From the body comes unconditional love and care.
The body is where we are experiencing it all...
spirit, emotion, intelligence, love, wonder, magic and
joy.

Breathe deep into the body.
Release what isn't yours.
Allow.

Meditate to develop your sanctuary so
that it can serve your joy.

Meditation allows the truth to
calm and release the body.

NOTES

NOTES

NOTES

Printed in Great Britain
by Amazon

45372154R00047